The Golden Measure of a True Lover

Love, Romance and the Divine Plan

Olusola O. Dada

PublishAmerica
Baltimore

© 2006 by Olusola O. Dada.
All rights reserved. No part of this book may be reproduced, stored in a retrieval system or transmitted in any form or by any means without the prior written permission of the publishers, except by a reviewer who may quote brief passages in a review to be printed in a newspaper, magazine or journal.

First printing

ISBN: 1-4241-1485-3
PUBLISHED BY PUBLISHAMERICA, LLLP
www.publishamerica.com
Baltimore

Printed in the United States of America

This book is dedicated to my pastors,
who taught me how to reach deep within myself
and to flow with God:

Pastor Olanrewaju Ijiwola
Rev. Kayode Ijisesan
Pastor Dotun Oragbade

And more importantly
to Jesus Christ, my Lord and Savior.

Acknowledgements

I would like to extend my appreciation and gratitude to the following people:

Victor Oshin, for helping with typing part of my first draft.

The staff of St. Anthony Park Home, for their enthusiasm and support of my poetry.

I love you all.

The Making of a Poet

Everybody has gifts. God has given every individual on the face of the planet a unique talent or gift. Our talents are meant to draw people to God, not to draw people away from God. Our gifts are meant to bless humanity and show the world God's diversity. God loves diversity and that is why He gave us different gifts.

Our gifts and talents are meant to draw us together without any regard for race, background or gender. It might take you a while to discover your talent—what God actually made you to do. Once you have discovered it, start running with the dream. Do not let anyone discourage you. At times friends and family might not understand you because you are not rising to their expectations. Do not let that bother you; just give everything you have to develop your talent.

I did not know that I was gifted in poetry until I took my first poetry class in college. After taking the class for a few weeks, I started to love poetry and I felt like it was just a part of me because the poems flowed out easily from within me, just like a flowing river.

I was very glad because I had tried to discover for what I was made for a very long time. I can only describe my experience with two verses from my first official poem:

> I have found myself in poetry;
> Poetry has found itself in me.

I grew up with pastors whose preaching inspired me. Therefore, my poems are meant to inspire people wherever they are. My mission is to write poems that both teens and adults can easily understand and relate to. This is why I choose words that are very easy to understand. Whenever you study any of the poems, do not just read everything at once. Study the poems line by line and try to understand or appreciate the words chosen to explain my ideas.

Read it very slowly and use the dictionary to find the meaning of some words. This will enhance your understanding of my poems. We are all very poetic. Poem is one of the attributes of God. If you study the scriptures, you will find numerous and amazing poems from Genesis to Revelation.

It is amazing that both believers and unbelievers can write and create poems. Poetry is a part of us because we are made in the image of God and God Himself is very poetic. If you have surrendered your life to Christ, reading, writing, reciting, singing and thinking about poems can be an act of worship.

At times, a word that you might need to get through a

very difficult time may show up in a poem. Sometimes poems give me the encouragement and the inspiration that I need to keep going when I feel like quitting.

Godly poems are very fascinating. They draw you closer to God. When you need to make a very difficult decision, you might find something in a poem that will give you the green light. When you read and think about a poem, you might get some ideas that you've never thought about before.

According to Joel Osteen's "Everybody Needs Encouragement" (October 17, 2004, broadcast), we all need something or somebody to encourage us from time to time. At times, writing or reading a poem might be the best way to deal with feelings of loneliness, sadness, or anger. It is very easy to pour out your emotions into poetry. I personally think that it is one of the best coping mechanisms when our emotions hit the roof. We can divert the boiling energy to write, and you would be amazed at the beauty of your poems.

We learn from the scriptures that our attention is to be focused on things that are lovely, pure, true, noble, right, admirable, praiseworthy (Philippians 4:8 Niv). These seven qualities will all be beautifully displayed in the poems in this book.

My poems are designed to inject life into distress, to show the goodness of nature, to appreciate the good things that God has blessed us with, and to bring us into an intimate relationship with the Creator.

I know that there are many poems out there. Some of the poems focus on anger, loneliness, sadness and lust. But the poems in this book focus on celebrating life and displaying God's design for humanity. The poems will lift up your spirit and lead you back to the Creator—the greatest poet that has ever been.

Isn't it interesting to really know God as a writer? My focus in this book is to write poems that will inspire people everywhere. God is the first and the best inspirational poet and writer. Because of His love, He sent Jesus to take our place in the world. Jesus died a painful death so that you will not have to face a painful death. Jesus fought and won the victory over diseases so that you will not have to carry a single trace of deadly disease or any form of sickness in your body. We all have sinned, but Jesus came and exchanged His righteousness for our sins so that we could stand righteous before God. Jesus became poor (if you compare what He had on earth to what He had in heaven) so that you do not have to live in poverty.

What would you do if someone told you that He would take all your sickness and disease, and you would not have to go for a single doctor's visit throughout your lifetime. That is exactly what Jesus did, and that is what my poems are about. Poems communicate experiences and feelings that are very difficult to express with words in a unique way. I have read some poems that are very hard to understand. I could not find a clue to what the poems are about. The wordings in those poems are such that you will need a dictionary to understand every single line in the poem. Those poems are boring because the readers cannot connect with the experience that is being communicated. Hence, I have made the poems is this book very simple and easy to understand.

Jesus is the best motivational speaker I have ever known. A lot of speakers will try to motivate you from outside to inside, but Jesus will motivate you from the inside out. Jesus is willing to exchange His strength for your weakness. Why don't you consider turning your life to him now? Ask Him to forgive you your sins and come into your heart and lead you in the right direction in life. He is ready to fill you with His joy and His peace that passes all understanding. I can feel His joy in my heart because I gave Him the invitation.

Natural Love

I know your strength,
And your weaknesses;
Since you are the
Love of my life,
I've found a greater
Passion for you.

My life assignment is
To help you discover
The giants behind
Your strength and ability,
And to help you
Find the antidote to
Your weaknesses;

Even though I
Understand my own frame
I shall never quit
Helping you excel.

The Only One

Many girls passed through
My eyes;
But none entered
My mind:

From school to work
From work to library
From friends to family

You are the glue
That holds my life
Together,

From the first time
Our four eyes met,
Your eyeballs entered
My brain,

And my whole world
Stood still—

I couldn't break down
My feelings
Until I realized that we
Were divinely hooked.

The Cool Love

I've got a passion,
A passion for something greater,
Something much higher
Than I could ever imagine,

Many have experienced love,
Many have placed
Their life support in
Romance,

But I present to
You the most attractive
And the best relaxation kingdom:
God's heart beating
Against my heart
God's spirit massaging
My bones like a
Professional message therapist.

My body and destiny
Enjoying the nourishment
Of the golden life;
The life of Jesus
Gently calming and
Cooling my veins.

Discovering a True Lover

Moving away from the
Car, I headed toward
The club's entrance.
I had just returned from the war.

Entering the crowded club,
A model-like lady
Flashed a single smile at me.
I replied with a triple smile.

She seemed so nice and
Ruthlessly charming; her
Nose, eyes, cheek and long hair
Were perfect, and just as
If she was ingeniously designed
By the Creator.

She was attracted to me
And I felt the same way about her.
We became close friends and
We eventually tied the knot.

After 12 months, she started
Showing her true colors;
Little did I know that I
Had just signed my joy away.
I did not realize that
She was a gold digger.
The first question she asked
After our union was,
How much treasure have
You got?
And where do you keep
Them all?

Had I known, I
Wouldn't have signed my joy away.
She seemed to be honest
And perfect.
My two eyes had deceived me.
The momentum of our divorce
Shattered my emotions.

I've learned the lesson
Of a lifetime:
If I were to marry again,
I would marry someone
Who has a heart for Christ.

(This poem is based on the true-life story of my very close friend.)

A New Identity

There was a time
I was disillusioned;
I didn't know what
to do or where to go.
    I went to school,
        had friends and a loving
        family, yet my personal
        Identity remained a mystery.

I started fellowshipping
at church,
I turned my life affairs
over to Jesus,
        He gave me a new dream
        and a golden passion,
        He gave me a new identity
        and a new hope,
        I finally found peace and
        and a lasting joy.

I've made a fresh discovery:
You are a unique being;
God made you with special
consideration and unique features.
    No man can perfectly
    duplicate your efforts
    because you're God's masterpiece,
    because you've got a God kind of life
    in you,
    because the Holy Ghost dwells
    in your spirit,
    Since the Greater One resides
    in your spirit,
    Since God has given you a
    unique and special personality.

A Rediscovery of My God-Given Gifts

My photographer had
Just taken my picture.
He showed me several
Of my posing images
And he asked me to
Choose the two
Better views.

I chose the one with
A standing posture,
And another one
With my head sideways.

He showed me the
Shots on the computer.
It had nothing
Short of a model figure.

Suddenly, my eyes
Were opened;
I realized the God
Had given me so
Many gifts that I
Wasn't even aware of.
Modeling can become

My lifestyle,
But not the usual type
Of models;
My class of modeling
Will always keep his
Clothes on,
And have nothing to do
With lust,
But have all to do with
My God-given cuteness
And style.

Again, I realize that
I have an attraction for
Nature's beauty by my
Innate structure.
I will not have a second
Thought about getting my
Own studio and manufacturing
Pictures that would change
Our world and my own world.

Thus, I have also been
Blessed with my ability
To command people's respect
With my writing skills.
All these assignments are
Part of me by my
Innate design,
But I've got to follow
My heart, step by step.

A Tribute to Faith Boosters

Someone believes in me
    When no one notices me,

Someone frames an image of the
    Best in me,
When no one believes in me.

Someone showers me
    With heavenly love
When many think nothing
    Good can come out of me.

Someone focuses on the best
    In me
When my peers focus
    On my weaknesses.

Someone gives me a reason
    To keep moving
When I've got a dozen of
    Reasons to quit.

Someone shows me
    My future talent,
When everything I ever
    Tried was a failure.

Someone cares when the whole
    World turns its back on me.

I salute your courage.

(First written for Rose Ndungu. Your words inspired me to produce this piece. Jan. 2005)

The True Measure of a Lover

One who is ready to love me for who I am
One who believes the best in me
One who is patient with my inadequacies
One who is willing to carry me when I am falling
One who listens to my ideas from time to time.
One who is willing to delay deep intimacy till marriage
One who is always willing to forgive.
One who doesn't just focus on my
Mistakes but is willing to help
Me find a cure
One who is willing to tell me the truth
Even when it feels painful
One who understands the Jesus kind
Of love

America and Compassion

America always rises up
With the airborne motion
Of a rocket,
And with a purple compassion,
Almost parallel to the passion
Of the Christ.

Nature has just unleashed
Her black and circular forces—
It's South Asia,
It's the tsunami,
Over 150,000 dead.
The heat of the turmoil
Ripped my soul apart.

The only true glance
of hope
rests in the hands of
nations around us,
And her people—
The pouring of relief
gold into the epicenter
of distress.

America stood up
Once again,
With the the wings
of her government
And with the gifted
courage of her people,
And together they
answered the higher
calling.

All partitioned nations
set aside their thorns
Once again
To pay tribute
to the grave,
To alleviate the anguish
of the survivors,
And to stand for a
better world.

An Attorney's Passion

The life of God glows
through my spirit being,
His nature lights me
from inside out,
His magnetic presence
draws me to the royal throne.

His anointing illuminates
my mind and body,
His radiance permeates
my entire being.
I suddenly realized that
the manifest presence of
the Holy One is real
and beyond measure.

I looked deep inside
to figure out the root
of my feeling and hungry
conscience;
I realized that I just gave
Jesus the POWER of ATTORNEY
over my life.

An Ounce of the Author's Personality

By my internal alignment,
I stay attracted
To creative phrases.
This might
Help explain my
Poetic expressions;
By the inner assembly of
My upper wires,

I stand attracted
To shining materials
And polished substances;
I love skillful blend of colors
With nature
Because my eyes
Enjoy its
Glorious beauty and
Sweet taste.

Beyond Your House (Winter)

Sitting behind my computer
Desk
In my fluorescent decorated
Room
I long for a taste of sunlight.

I envied the coolness
Of the outside world;
The filaments are
Spectators in my own home.

After a gentle walk by the lake,
My clumsy mind turned a
Creative problem shooter;

Thus we need two
Environments to
survive:

The inside world
And
The outside world

Freedom finally laughed
At me,
As the comfort of sunlight
Passed through me.

Fantasy

We all live in a world,
A world filled with
Fantasy and fun;

Some indulge in pornography,
Others love deep and unholy
Intimacy below the belt
Without a wedding ring.

For others, it is secular
Romance books
Filled with perverted love
And feet-height imagination.

These romance novels
Embrace physical bonding
In the absence of a holy union.
The lyrics are focused on self,
Me! Me! Me!

It is regrettable that many
Lives have been wounded
By the perverted images
Filled with dark love.

The ingenious Creator
Reveals that
Romance is more of giving
And less body fiction;
It is a mission to give your
Best resources, time and money.

Romance transcends physical
Touch to acts of service;
It is patient and willing to say
"I DO."

Feeling the Heat of the Music

I got up in the morning,
Prayed and ingested a
Little music into my soul.

I was ready to face
The heat and the severe
Snow that awaited me.

I stepped into my car
And tuned my radio
To a Christ-like station. …KTIS

I listened with ingenious
Patience as I drove; Holy Spirit's
Radiance cut through my bones.

The lyrics boosted up the courage
In me; I was fully saturated
To handle the blazing storm.

I got abundant energy
For the day; I was fully charged to
Handle the stress and the roaring life fire.

I finally found my life-support
In music; Christ-like music has
Found its soul in me.

From Lemon to Lemonade

When I pick up a lemon,
It's just another fruit;
When I squeeze it
For its juice,
The sour taste
Bites my tongue.

And when I turn it
Into lemonade,
All my five senses
Envy its taste.

My potential is sour
just like a circular lemon.
Like a gold mine with miners,
My potential wants to produce.

It is only the blue sky
that can praise the
creative sound
Buried within my
potential.

Ace of Aces

I found myself
    In a brand new world;
A new world has found
    Her way through me.

I've found my
    Writing sword;
I've embraced
    The poetry of light.

Getting Filled Up

I grew up in a big mansion.
My father heads the highest
Banking estate in the land.

I had access to college
And a better future.
Deep inside, I felt like
Something was missing—
It's not money or friends.

I felt like an empty pop can,
My heart was an empty
Gift box wrapped with
A huge gift wrap.

Suddenly, a friend introduced
Me to Jesus.
Suddenly, I gave Jesus the
Power of attorney over my life.

He moved in with the force
Of an ocean current
And filled me with a gentle
And slow motion.

I was joyfully filled;
His bright light chased
The darkness in my heart away
And my life became a written epistle.

Hidden Beauty

It's a pretty face,
It's the hot legs;
Chasing her is my
Current aspiration.

Like a model queen
She goes;
Like a police car
My eyes pick a chase.

The slimness of her
Body gives me an
Equation to solve.

Unknown to my mind
Is the wealth and
Authority of hidden beauty:

A beauty of two parallel hearts,
A mixture of two souls
That is blind to physical
View and spotless faces.

The value placed on only
The outside face
Will destroy any man.
I must not let my eyes
Be seduced by only her body.
Physical beauty fades,
But the radiance of her
Hidden beauty keeps
Drawing us closer every
Single day:

A beauty of Christ,
A beauty of unseen
Chemistry,
Whose root is devoid of
The physical realm,
Since it's only our
Hidden beauty as a couple
That can absorb the
Shocks and waves
Of marriage.

The Higher Creativity in Action

God dislikes homogeneity
But He enjoys creativity
And diversity;
why are there many races
in the world,
why are there many
Languages,
why do some boast as
if their language is
superior to any other language;

No one language or color
Is superior over another.
God loves to
See all languages displayed
In action—

The radiance of the
Spectrum of the rainbow,
The glorious sight of the
Alternating sunlight and
Moonlight,
The different dimensions
Of music:

"Ever tried to listen to same song
Track for ten straight days?"
The variation of every
Cell and drift,
The numerous voices
Of the birds,
The diverse gifts
Of the human mind
and body;

All admire one thing:
The ingenious mind
Of the Greater One.

Just a Date

They've just met in college,
They've been in contact for seven days.
Little did she know that he is a novice "player";
His friends had showed him how to
Lure and conquer.

He promised her a date,
But all she wants is love.
They both enjoy transient love
But in alternate dimensions.

She craves affection and attention,
He craved dark, secret passion.
She wants affirmation;
He is only interested in a fatal night.

In their two souls
They both wanted love
And love has fled their company.

Passionate love in the body
Only brings true joy
When both parties enter the
Room without a missing
Wedding ring.

His Breakthrough

It's at the park

It's at dawn

And vanished is the

Active and noisy crowd;

The trees lift up their hands

To praise God.

To God I raise my hands

Until worship takes me over;

And my problems melt away.

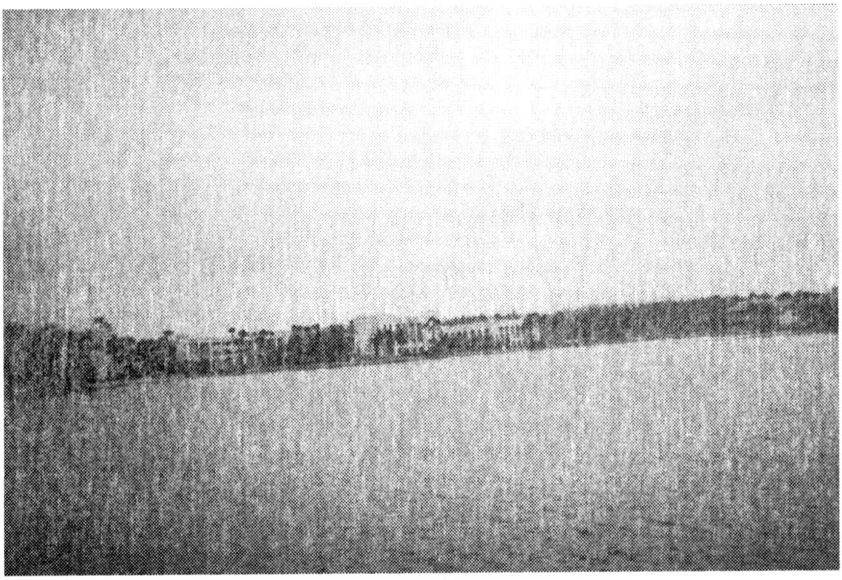

Knowledge and a Second Chance

She is only 17 years old.
    She got a job in the kitchen
And now she enjoys the tasks;
    She quits acquiring knowledge.

27 New Year's Eves came and left,
    She still works there,
But when an unseen and dark
    Storm hits the facility

The business was declared closed
    And never to be re-opened again.
Her hope and her physical destiny
    Became crushed.

She started crying in her secret closet:
    Had I known,
I wouldn't have stopped learning;
    Now my future seems to be stuck.

Love

Love is more than
A sweet word.

There is a sweet
In love;
There also exists
A fire
In love.

The sweet of love
Calms down my soul,
Yet the fire of love
Purifies my being.

Though painful and
Roaring we call them,
Both keep your head
And destiny under control.

Though harsh on my mind
And body it seems,
The end product is a purified
And eternally refined person.

Living Word

When the service ends,
I boost my Bible up and
I walk across the lobby
till I reach Living Word
Bookstore.

When I step in,
the dim light guides and
lures me to focus on the
life-transforming books.

When I walk in,
I see staff that radiate
Christ's glory through
their unique and lovingly
contagious attitudes;

They've got life and joy
diffusing through their
fresh and smiling
faces.

The books and music
that you help transfer
to other believers fuel
the drive for a better future;
only eternity can actually reveal
the magnitude of your service.

There is something unique
about the bookstore:
the staff are awesome,
their attitudes inspiring,
their smiles inject life
into hopelessness;

their enthusiasm cannot be
measured in words;
it is only the GREATER ONE
that can showcase the numerous
lives that have been loaded
with deliberate blessings.

Looking Deep

My men might betray
Me but they
Cannot kill my
Spirit—

My friends might
Oppose my success
But they cannot
Kill my dreams—

My family might
Disown me for a
Season but
Jesus would never
Abandon me for
A split second—

My boss might fire
Me but my innate
Skills would keep
Glowing in the dark—

My happiness may be
Ruined
But the holy joy
On my inside boils
With laughter—

I may be cut off
From my dreams
But the greater one
Living in me
Opens a second
Door before my eyes—

Lost and Found

Sitting in my room
    With my eyes focused
On the screen,
    As if my head was fixed,
My TV gave me a
    Praiseworthy look;
My heartbeat tripled
    With joyful rhythm.

I have found my innate
    Dreams in my heroes,
Yet the auditions have
    Eluded my being,
Since I possess none of
    Those skills.

The Oscar silences my soul,
    The Grammy makes my brain flip,
The bestsellers laugh at my script,
    The heavyweight cycle crushes
My spirit.

I finally caught a glimpse
    Of my joy in comedy;
Comedy rises up like an
    Inflated balloon
At the foot of my being.

From every axis of the nation,
    The fans yearn for my presence;
Wherever my mouth is opened,
    Others are inspired to open theirs
'til their jaws reach their chests.

Lovetea & Mobolaji

I found my HEART
In you;   ...Lovetea
I found my LIFE
    In you,   ...Mobolaji

Your strength is now
My strength;
And my peace
Your peace.

If I were to live twice,
I would still find
You,

Even with my two
Eyes closed.

The Scribe

My table is my
    Pen's backbone.

My chair and right
    Arm are
        My factory.

My mattress is my
    Pen's leisure center.

These resources inject
    Laughter and life
        Into my script.

Love is Not Blind

I am only 23 years old.
    I've got a fat-pocket job
With a brand new porch.
    I have many friends.

My family's love is genuine.
    I have access to anything I want
And now in my own apartment
    I crave for diverse girls.

I score several touchdown points.
    The ladies enjoy my company.
I lure them into my dark bedroom
    Without any wedding ring.

On a Friday morning
    Leaving the doctor's office
Tears drop down my eyes
    Because I will never be the same.

I hadn't thought that
    Life will shoot its arrows at me
Because of the chronic
    Sexually-diffused disease.

With only a few years to live
    Tears gallop down my face
And I realize that the condom
    Was destined to fail.

With my family close to my last bed
    And my friends holding my hand
My head rolls to the right
    As my spirit flees my body.

Looking down on my lifeless body
    My family and friends mourn my demise
Never again will I enjoy the dark intimacy
    That cut my life short.

If I were to come back
    To life again
I would seek intimacy
    With only my wife.

Had I known,
    I would have deferred
Passionate romance
    Till I met my wife.

I should have followed
    My pastor's example.
If anyone can hear me now,
    Do not copy my stupid lifestyle.

More than the Fourth

It's the fourth of July;
I see balloons rising up
Into the sky
In colors of green, white
And blue
And victory parades going
On from city to city.

The energy of the
Inflated balloons flows
Through me;
Yet the balloons are part of me.

I see myself rising
With the balloons
Without any regard
For the law of gravity.

With one mission
And one purpose,

With one dream
And one perseverance,

The topmost sky
Is just the beginning,
The beginning of my
Appointed success,
A partial fulfillment
Of my utmost destiny.

Nature by Design

Celebrating the beauty of
His creation,
I lowered my neck three times.

The light of the moon was designed
to reflect my shadows;
The radiance of the rainbow was
carefully structured;
the shape of the earth was perfect
for its contents.

The rain was selected to water
our farmland;
We've got natural gold so we can
appreciate heavenly texture
and sip a taste of the glory.

We've got heartwarming pets
And singing sparrows
so we can love others without
any attached strings
And lift our voices to
Welcome the Holy One.

We've been showered with sunlight;
We don't have to walk in gross darkness
or lack food on the table.

The trees shed their clothing in fall
but always get new clothing in spring.
The radiant green leaves reveal the inner
character of the trees.

All these functions have been
Authored by the Greater One
Whose ingenious mind cannot be matched.

Looking Right

When you walk into a store,
All you want is just to buy, shop, and leave.
But there is a store I must never forget:
Northwestern is the golden name.
When I walk in, I see dreams come true;
When I step in, I find books and music that inspire
me to succeed.

When I show up, I find contagious workers
who are always willing to help.
Northwestern is more than
just a bookstore to me;
Here I find artistes who deliver the gospel
message with humor, intensity and courage.

Whenever I am lonely and I want to do something,
I step into the car and I navigate the road until
I reach the store.
Then I find great books and DVDs
that fill my time.

Where can I find a store like Northwestern?
When I step in,
I meet cheerful and loving staff;
When I walk in,
I find uplifting music and books.

Northwestern is more than a bookstore to me;
She delivers life and energy,
She delivers hope for dreams come true.
She is like a magnet to believers,
And I will always remember her.

Not for the Unmarried

Looking into his eyes,
She covets a hug,
But he is only
Interested in something
Beyond his boundaries.

Like an experienced hunter
He tricks her;
Like a team without a coach,
She falls for him.

Had she known, she
Would not have given in,
Because he's only interested
In having his way.
His mouth utters sweet
Roses but deep in his
Heart he's only interested
In one night
Even though he knows that
He's in a dead-end relationship.

He leaves her conscience scarred
And her emotions confused.
All she wanted was
Acceptance and affection.
The truth is sleeping
Parallel and deep affection
Are two different realities.
He wants the initial and
She wants the latter.

Had she known, she
Wouldn't have allowed
Him to define what
The separate realities mean.
She finally ended up
With discomfort, pain and shame.
When she suddenly came to herself
She remembered an easy
Escape route is to find
People who passed
Through the same route
Without doing it,
And
Invest time and energy
In their books.

Pay Day

Life is full of revenge;
Not a
Revenge by man

But a revenge
Provoked
By breaking His will
And
His design for man.

Teenagers lying parallel
With each other,
Without wedding rings.

Unmarried men and women,
Entertaining impurity
In their bodies.

So incurable diseases
Destroyed many
Of them and tore apart
Their lives.

The pain of a broken
Fellowship with
The Creator of the universe
Is unbearable.

But God is still
Mindful of
Healing your body
And
Your spirit;

Only if you will
Surrender all
To Jesus

The Popular Girl

Why die to be popular
When you can be beautiful;

Why make popularity your
Aim
When you are so gifted;

Why focus on the admiration
Of many friends
When there is a genius
Spirit inside you;

Why measure your worth
By the opinion of others
Rather than the joy inside you.

Popularity has been discovered
By many

To give you the needed attention
But no personal devotion,
To give you unknown friends,
But no words of inspiration.

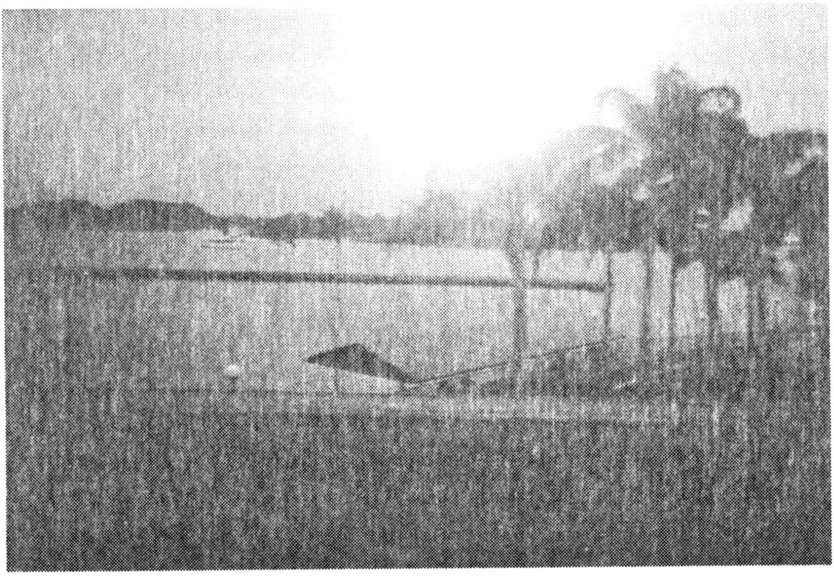

Pretty Faces Fade

Stay in Love
Fall in Love
Fall out of Love

Like a bestselling novel
He studies "pretty faces"

Why should a man follow
A woman,
Just because of her spotless,
Soft and magnetic face alone.

Only one thing is real—
Such a man is only
Interested in one night,
He is only interested in
Breaking her heart,
Since he is surrounded
By a dark and a novice mind

Her self-esteem is twisted
His knowledge of the Holy One
Is empty

So many men have been
Ruined by pretty faces
And hot legs;
To stay in love is to connect
At the unseen realm,
Heart to heart.

Beauty is good
But only when two separate
hearts are
Mingled.

Refined by Trial

Living in her father's
Small and enlarged
    House,
        She fights
Dark tornadoes
In her innermost
Parts with her unseen boxing
Gloves.

The perverted poverty
Taught her how to be
Content with anything.
The constant struggle
Between her and her
Parents helped refine
    Her character;
    The heat of
Her underground
And emotional battles
Make her reach for Jesus.

The more she uncovered
Scriptural solutions,
The more deadly her
Challenges became;
She was finally refined
By fire.

When the fire changed
Into a cold and
    Calm lake,
    She admits:
Tough struggles never last
But patient and stylishly
Spiritual
People do.

Singles and Teenagers

Why do some people
Place high value on dignity?
Why can't I just have fun like
My other friends?

After all, the TV always confirms
Bonding of uncovered bodies.

My best buddy is always anti-fun.
"Christ-minded believers have a better
plan," he says.

If you have joined yourself with
the "Greater One,"
There is the Holy Ghost always
willing to help you make smart
choices.

I feel the same hormone pressure
from within just like you;

But I've got to listen
to the Master's voice;
Since He is my life coach
And a coach knows better
than a player.

I've got the best contract
in the whole world:

His prosperity for
    my obedience;
His strength for
    my weakness;
My abstinence till marriage
    for His success;
My purity for a life
    without chronic disease.

And with all these benefits;
Why wait to sign a contract
with the Holy One?

Standing Upright

She is only a
Freshman in college;
Her mother wants
Her to put
More resources into learning.

I want to go
Play with my
Friends, she says,
But her mum's
Mind is already fixed.

You're only allowed
To socialize for three hours
After class,
Then you can invest
More hours into your
Future, says the mother.

It summertime,
All my friends are partying;
Why should I even
Waste my time
Talking to you?
The girl roared.

Honey, the mother replied,
I walked out on my
High school education
Just before graduating;
And without two jobs,
I cannot stand
On my feet.
I want you standing upright
With fewer
Than two jobs.

The Chosen One

Many men have crossed
My path
But you stand out
In my mind

Many men passed me by
On your mum's wedding
Night,
But you are the chosen one
Appointed to give me
A ride home,

A ride that changed
Our lives forever.

Once our paths crossed,
Now we're closer than
Our siblings.

Though I'm a beauty queen
Your straight personality
And cool heart gives me
A double love for you.

Your constant gifts
Stir up the joy within me
And walk through my emotions.

Your thoughtfulness about
My three sisters breaks down
My wall.

The Dirty Prince

She is only eighteen;
She loves her boyfriend
But his mind is crude;

He's not ready for
Commitment.
He is only interested
In the juice
And not in the fruit.

Her brain is as blank
As his.
They made a baby
Without thinking about
The process and the ending.

The guy disappeared,
Never to be seen again
In his city.
Lonely and depressed,
She withdrew to herself.

Had I known,
I wouldn't have shared
My apartment with him
Till I'm found with my
Wedding ring.

The Double Assignment

She is only two years
Short of being considered
An adult in the eyes of the law;

She has only one family bond—
Her mother.
Mother is a hardworking and strong
Lady.
She kisses her girl goodbye
Every morning before
She hits the road,

Only to return an hour
Before midnight.
She is already dreaming
On her bed by the time
Mum steps into the house.

Mother is tired of working two
Jobs just to make ends meet;
Had I known, I wouldn't have
Divorced him,
I should have stuck with him
Through thick and thin;

My dark freedom has deprived
Me of quality time with
My daughter.

I have given her all the costly
Gifts I have,
Yet our relationship is still in
The yellow zone.

She is getting raised by her
Teachers, her peers and the
Media but without my
Deep affection.

I have therefore resolved
To cast all my burdens on
Jesus;
And to let Him
Show me the best way to
Finish the journey.

The End of May

Standing by Lake McCarron
On a sunny Thursday,
The sun diminishing,
My mind starts to expand.

The lake is surrounded
By green and motionless creatures,
We call them trees.

The whiteness of the sky
Accepts the purity of
The dancing and flying birds.

The lake feels alive
Yet all her green
And strong security
Guards are still active.

I wondered why this is so,
But while gazing into the sky
The life in the sun entered
My own life through my eyes.

The answer to my question
Found me:
God's spirit is just like
The sun,
Giving us all the reason and
Energy to carry on

When all our strength
And purpose
Seem crushed.

The English Instructor

In my first English
    Class at Century,
She showed up with
    A couple of books;

A familiar face,
    And a brilliant
Code of ethics
    For the class.

Her narration
    Was wide and sharp.
Her chosen examples
    Stuck to my wandering brain.

The wordings were
    Direct and cheerful.
Free, fresh and fascinating
    Was her advancing dialect.

Her laughter lit up
    The students' faces;
Her presence was a cycle
    Between being strict and carefree.

So many classes have
    Come and gone,
Yet her unique charisma
    Still glows in my mind.

Many prefer their first
    Names but she draws
Attention to her
    Last name—Wu

Since it's easier
    For students to recollect.
The rhythm of her first name
    Gives my tongue a twisted focus.

Life is immersed in
    Diverse experiences
But some will always
    Stay glued to the mind.

If I were to start college
    A second time, I would
Choose her because she is
    Stylishly outstanding.

The Giant Behind Our Imagination

The brain is as crude
As a raw talent;
He needs to be explored
And enhanced.

The brain encloses several
Hidden files;
He functions like
Computer software.

The files need to
Be opened, then you
Can uncover your
Buried genius ideas.

The mind is the voice
Of the brain;
It has unlimited potential,
Like a new football recruit.

When the mind is properly
Fed and creatively utilized,
When you care enough to
Pen down your simple ideas,

You're preparing yourself
As a world-class genius;
You're giving yourself
The blessing of a lifetime.

The muscles of the mind
Rise and expand like a
Balloon filled with air,
When the mind is properly
Utilized.

The mind divides:
The rich and the poor,
The educated and the illiterate,
The whole and the disabled.

The mind births: both
Restrained and famous phrases.
The content of the heart is
Revealed by the brain's voice.

Only if you will care enough
To discover the fresh and
Concealed ideas
One day at a time.

The Man is Worth His "Queen"

He is only a few years
Older than a teenager.
He keeps his head upright
And his shoulders straight
Without any sense of guilt.

None of his five friends are
married,
Though they are almost
in their mid-twenties.
But they are all "players."
They enjoy the forbidden
apple;
They want a taste of every
Girl they meet.

But he had resolved to
Keep his mind pure,
His eyes sharp
Yet well-disciplined
By the cool truth
of the scriptures.
But his friends play
The torture game with

him:
Aren't you a man like us?
We love to have fun!
Why do you keep depriving
yourself of all the pleasure?
Everybody is doing it!

He looks straight into
their eyes:
Though I've prayed for you,
I still have a better deal than
Yours,
Till you reverse your choices.

With God I have a signed
Contract:
His Son's life for my
surrender and new awakening;
His mercy for my sins;
His cold and calm peace
for my troubled soul;
His graceful "Queen"
For my wife.

And all these are my
destiny
Only if I watch my steps
by His advice,
And when I hold my body
Till marriage.

The Touch of Life

There are different
Faces of touch:
There is the touch
Of a mother;
There also exists
The touch of a lover.

The touch of a friend
Is heartwarming;
The touch of a brother
Keeps your life together;
But there is a touch
That ranks above all others:

Some call it
The touch of life.
If you're struck by
This touch,
Any broken piece
Of your life assembles
Together,
You step into
A supernatural lifestyle.

When you're alarmed
By this touch,
Your life becomes
Saturated with the
Anointing.

Jesus Christ becomes
Genuine and greater
In your life;
Thus, the touch of life
Triumphs over the touch
Of death.

The Treasure in Books

The hunger for books can
Never be quenched,
Books written by men and women;
People crave for new ideas.
At times, the intensity
Of the ideas transform
Our lives.

As Amy Grant held a
Book in her hand,
The hidden rhythms and melodies
Brought her down on
Her knees
With a sacred passion
For God.

Likewise in my early teenage years,
With my literate
Grandmother I lived.
I found a red book
With a razor volume.

Opening the book to
A few pages beyond the
Middle page,
I read with undermined patience.
After a few minutes
Into the book,
I stepped into my
Secret closet,
Lifted up dirty hands
And I worshipped God.

I felt a strong and
A gentle cyclone engulfing
My head and shoulders.

I became visually and
Soulfully Christ-like.
My dirty hands
Became holy hands.
Jesus suddenly became
My Source and my Master.

A decade after this
Encounter with the supernatural book
A three-word headline
Stays plastered to my memory:
"World Bible School"

(Note: Amy Grant is a renowned gospel artist.)

The Two Parts of the World

Growing into a teenager,
His abode was the dark continent
Which is engulfed in a shadow;
When he faced his adult life,
He switched to the fluorescent
Saturated continent.

In the dark end,
His laughter was perceived
As a symbol of weakness.
At the light end,
His smile was a magnetic field
That lit up the faces of others
And turned enemies into friends.

The True Measure of a Man

One who is willing to forgive
One who is ready to protect
And feed the family at any cost
One whose heart is open to constructive
Criticism from wife
One who is slow to anger
One who has found victory in giving
Rather than receiving
One who always lead the family toward
Jesus
One who is willing to instill genuine morals
And godly values in the kids
One who is willing to acknowledge his mistakes
And seek forgiveness
One who always finds ways to build his
Kids' confidence.

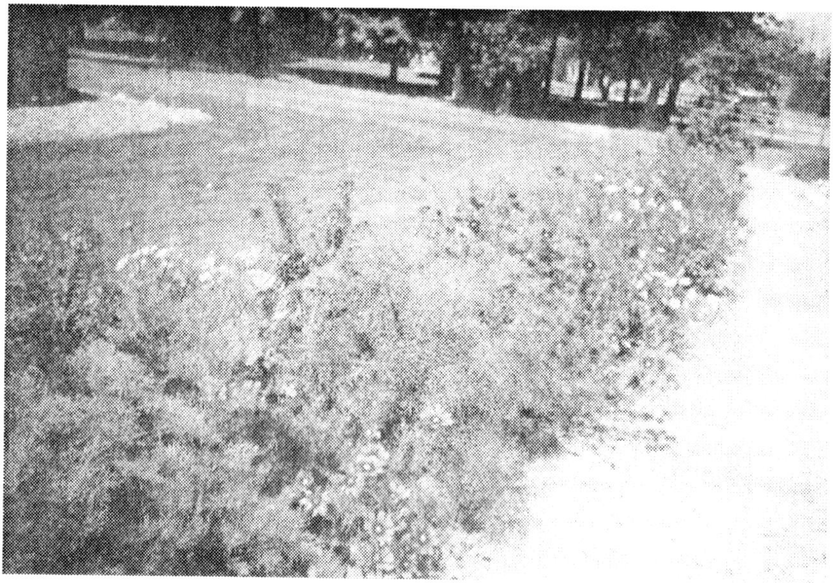

The Single Life

We long for a broad face
With our teeth vibrating;
We enjoy the right mood.

Yet singleness is a choice,
A choice to stand for good
Or evil;

A willingness to rise
To the standard and manual
Of the first manufacturer

That designed
Our body
And uniqueness.

The Undiluted Vow

Visiting with a
Family friend, two unmarried
brothers

Still in their twenties
Watched
Bright images on
The flat screen.

The man of the
House asked
The elder brother
A deep soul and
Crude question—
Are you still
A virgin?

He replied
"Yes" before the
Elderly man finished
The unusual question;
It was not easy
But I've been passionately
Protecting my slippery heart.

I have been swallowing
The right holy words into
My spirit;
I have been fellowshipping
With like-minded believers;
I do not think twice
About fleeing the scene
Of temptation.

Lastly, I've turned my
Eyes away from perverted
Information sources and images;
I study books
Written by Christ-like
Authors who cherish
Undiluted marriage.

Two Girlfriends

Two ladies grew up
In the same town.
They were close to
Each other
But their lives moved
In opposite lanes.

Jessica was as hot
As a model.
She craved shining
Cars and diamond-like outfits.
Her facelift gave her
A spotless baby face
And she enjoyed the company
Of multiple lovers.

Sharon was filled with
Internal beauty.
Even though Miss World
Was filled with jealousy for her
Sharon had inner joy which
Shone through her outfits,
Since her confidence and hope
Was placed in Jesus.
She shared one set of
Wedding rings with her man;
She inspired her offspring
And others to excellence.

Jessica's life became
A misery;
Her depression kept
Rolling downhill.
She became a
Candidate for suicide,
Since outer beauty fades.

Uniting America

Many have said, "She will not survive";
But she survived a bloody civil war:
United we stand, divided we fall.

Some say, "She will not last";
But she outlasted them all:
They all lowered their hats
in her honor.

Right wing and left wing, they say.
But both came from the source,
Both emerge from the same manufacturer.

Have you ever heard a brother
tell his sister, "You're not part
of my family because we just
had a quarrel"?

But the truth of the matter is
Blood is thicker than water;
It is only by tolerating each other
that we can find a lasting peace
and enjoy a diamond lifestyle.

America has always been
One Nation Under God,
The light and salt of the earth.
Many have given their lives for
her prosperity
because we're bound by one
constitution, one faith and
One Creator.

Waiting is Golden

We all need to work,
    Yet some jobs seem
To be more easy than others.
    Entering my client's room,
The television flashes two
    Transparent red images
At me.
    A hot feminine model and
Her prince charming swallowing
    Each other alive.

My romantic engine rose
    From silent to noisy;
My heartbeat tripled,
    My flesh cried for intimacy,
Yet my contract with
    God is Real

I am bound by my oath:
    He supplies me His divine
Health and the reply is my bodily
    Innocence.
We had already exchanged our gifts:

My iron for His gold,
My prayers for His angels,
My purity for His healing;

His love for my depression,
His covenant for my lust,
His radiance for my loneliness;

His chronic-disease-free jacket for
My abstinence,
His comfort and strength for
My waiting till marriage.

Watch Right

Watching the TV
In his big living room,
The fatal images give
Him a funny look.

All he wants to watch
Is just an action movie
But the movie
Turns into a naked body.

He has been battling
This for four years.

The information sources
Pay no attention;
They are only interested
In the profit.

The dark, perverted images
Keep distorting his mind;
Even when he is in the
Heart of prayer,
The images keep
Showing up.

The dark images
Are about to destroy him,
Because she brings hidden
Emotions to the surface.

His fiancée is about
To desert him,
Because he can't
Control his urges.

Suddenly his internal eyes are
Opened,
And he realizes that
He should have controlled
His external eyes
By watching the right things,
Because the eyes control
The mind;
The mind controls the
Usual but untimely aroused urges.

A Gift for God

Her voice sounds
Like a joyful sparrow;
The golden sunset
Wants a glimpse of her hair,
Magnetically radiant
And exceptionally
Natural.

Her height attracts men
With bold masculinity.
Miss Universe wants to
Be like her.

She is unlike her friends;
She is uniquely gifted,
Yet she uses her ingenious
Gift to magnify God.

Her pastor respects her,
The congregation loves
To be around her;
She commands the attention
Of the world
Because she draws them toward
Jesus.

Changing

From one relationship to another
From boyfriend to boyfriend
From girlfriend to girlfriend
From marriage to out-
Of-marriage

From a divorced status
To a remarried status

Circumstances change from year to year
Finances changes from summer to spring
Working environment changes
Your best friend
Changes from time to time

Why keep your hope and
Trust in something that
Is unstable

When you can trust in the stable
And constant

Why allow your heart to
Be broken into pieces
When you can have a
Flourishing and lively heart

Why allow your emotions
To plunge into depression
When you can have the
Greatest inspirational speaker
That ever lived in your heart

His name is the
Prince of Peace
He wants to introduce Himself
To you

I am Jesus Christ
I died on the Cross
For you,
When you put your hope
And trust in Me,
You will never be
Disappointed

I came so you can have
A golden life
Give Me your lemons
And I will help you
Turn them into lemonade
Only if you would trust Me

Allow Him in your heart
And He will fill your
Mouth with cake
And your soul with joy

Your joy will accelerate
Your patience
And patience will help
You withstand the
Advancing tornado

And your destined
Wife will show up
Your destined husband
Will eventually emerge.

Beyond Summer

Driving through my
neighborhood,
The naked trees give
me a stunning look.

Their clothing and
glory is lost for a season,
And not to return
Till the next season.

Thrilled teenagers driving
on a dry and rocky lake,
Even with the intensity
of the sun,
The lake remains solid.

The coolness of the
atmosphere makes
my brain think.
Yet, the silent force
of the air dries up
my flesh.

Excited

They feel empowered
Because they've got a
Bigger body and
A fuller chest.

As some say, babies
Having babies.

Thirteen and fifteen years old,
Wanting to have babies.

Some imagine, "After all,
I've got a boyfriend
And we can have all
The fun we want.
I can do whatever I
Like with my body."

But the fact is
The boyfriend is not
Willing to stick with you;
He is only interested
In having fun.
Why are you so cheap?

Why are you so blind to love?
Why would you want to raise two kids
By you working two jobs?

You deserve better than that;
You deserve a loving
Husband and not a cheap
Boyfriend. God will eventually
Bring him across your path
At the right time.

You're God's offspring.
He designed your body.
He wants the best
For you.

He designed your
Body to function better
With a wedding ring glued to
One of your fingers,

So your body can
Be disease-resistant,
So you can be free from
Ungodly shame and regret.

If you've surrendered
Your life and life routines
To Jesus on your knees,
He is ready to forgive you
And fill the loneliness
In your heart
If only you will ask Him.

Stronger than Love

Valentine's is near:
Couples holding hands
As their faces rejoice.

And I am filled with
Persistent joy
Since I'm still single.

"Who will you date by next Valentine's?"
A friend inquired.
I don't need one
Till I'm ready for
A commitment,
My voice replied.

Romance is good
Yet a relationship
With Christ is awesome
And warm.
Intimacy in romance will
Soon fade
Yet a fellowship with
Christ cools my soul 24/7.

When intimacy with Christ
Is placed on the same scale
As intimacy with flesh,
The heart of Christ will
Always triumph.

But you can enjoy
Both facets of courtship
If only you will make
Your date with Jesus
More frequently than any
Other human contacts;
And my single mind
Kept intact

Till I'm prepared
For marriage.

Determined

To the tune of the
Supervisors,
The employees dance.

And to the blessing
Of our Creator,
We maintain our purity.

To the orders of the
Doctor,
The citizens rejoice.

To the words of our
God,
We keep the marriage bed clean

Till we dive into our holy union
And the holy abundance
Overtakes us.

When we take a stand for
Him
To reject the popular

And to obey the divine,
Our lives become
Written epistles,

Read by the mind of
The unsaved
Yet admired and revered

By the whole world.